Dedicated to folks who live on the edge... and daring to live
a dream skiing or new business... or in some case both...

A book about business and the art of skiing?

Either activity involves potential for both great pain and great joy.

As a lifestyle skier and serial entrepreneur the similarities of mindset and execution required to excel at either is increasingly clear.
I hope to share my passion for both... and per image hope it lends a "hand" for inspiration.

To the books contributors– you truly embody the art of business and ski at every level.

For every shot published by these folks they commit countless hours of "business" and core execution of the qualities we discuss in this book... for this ....
Thank you. Please visit their websites

Business and the art of ski

Photo Dave Thomas operations manager www.baldface.net Baldface Lodge Snowcat Skiing

If you aren't sure this is an image of great joy...

Even a 100 years ago
the practice of skiing
or running your own
business was not a
lifestyle option – it was
necessity... At one time
we were all business
people - we plotted,
farmed, hunted,
succeeded and failed at
our own hands and by
our own designs. Over
time cities blossomed
"workers" became
more prevalent and the
"business owner" rarer.

Flash forward - the
speed of advancing
technology and product
is allowing for new
businesses to launch
and compete like never
before... and the leisure

skier emerged to ride increasingly technical skis for no reason other than it is wicked fun and we can ~ leaving behind the original skier who only skied & risked life ...to get from A to B.

It's a Whole New World...

And like those who peer through the tips of their skis to the bottom of a run, wave dismissively at friends shouting "insanity" and launch down the double black ski run anyway - launching a business is not for the weak of heart.

But it can be fun .

Shoot QR to visit photographer site

Set it up...
Evolve

Ski & Starts Ups

Photo: Francois Marseille: action sport photographer based in BC Kootenays http://goo.gl/CR3Ms

The thumbnail is Olaus Jeldness who hosted some world record ski parties in 1847 + in Rossland BC home to the longest running winter carnival in N. America in his memory (110 yr +) This Kootenay region skis!

To ski or not to ski... launch or not?

Difficult, cold, disheartening, painful, expensive, frustrating, soul and gut wrenching, the cause of sleepless nights and general body and headaches.

And yes we are talking about being self employed. Skiing is the same but with potential foot pain of which you will hopefully never feel again.

There can be glory and it does get easier ...some say it can even become addictive

...like the art of skiing.

"I do not believe a man can ever leave his business. He ought to think of it by day and dream of it by night."

—Henry Ford

Photo: Dave Thomas skier, snowcat operations manager and more... visit his gallery

"Commitment unlocks the doors of imagination, allows vision, and gives us the "right stuff" to turn our dreams into reality."

—James Womack

Commitment

There will be many times in these activities when you have to commit. There is the undercurrent of commitment that moves us every day like each turn we make on the hill. Then there are the bigger commits ; like a new product, investment or big terrain feature. Failure to commit will lead to failure to perform.. pure and simple.

The photo in this section is one of my favorite examples of both skiing and business commitment. This is commitment to get the shot. For both the skier and the photographer... they wanted an exceptional shot, the consequences were significant, they made a business and sport decision to proceed. They ran scenarios, creating diligence to mitigate the risks and optimize the outcomes and when the time came they committed.

A failure of either party to commit at this moment would have been suffice to say; foundation for a very negative outcome – but they stuck it ...and a great "product" was born.

Photographer: Christian Pondella. Yes that is his boot at the bottom of the photo. Commitment = yes … www.christianpondella.com or for more shoot QR code

Confidence

Partner of commitment, welling up from the heart, mind and soul Confidence is the essence that knows... this is going to work.

Experience is not the only source.. When a skier drops a line for the first time – the confidence in reaching the bottom alive may lie in their experience as a skier -but that is no different than saying I am a good code writer so my software will succeed.

There is the environment, features, endurance, ability to react to the unexpected, testing the conditions, knowing your gear is solid... and a dash of faith.

Likewise in business planning, strategize, learn/train with others (mentors, coaches etc) know your environment, your launch, your goals et al.. When you are ready to take the leap be bold...

Whatever it takes for you to have confidence.. source it out, use it and share its power

Christian Pondella and skier taking confidence to a new level
www.christianpondella.com

Vision

Vision to see the where the untracked opportunities might lie in some overlooked niche of trees.

Vision to see the big picture of where your group is, who is lagging, who may need help so everyone excels.

Peripheral Vision to see competition coming to poach your line and the vision to figure out how to get there first (or get out of the way)

Can it be learned ?

Yes - like learning to ski- unable to see the line, following others examples or boldly pushing ahead until suddenly - THERE IT IS!

The line between the trees or the moguls or the leverage in a business strategy ..is suddenly just THERE...so obviously there.. and it will never be the same again.

Be diligent, practice it and the vision will come.

Skiing tips:
1. If you can't see... Head into the trees – the shortened distance allows your brain to get from turn to turn with tree landmarks. Similarly in business ..create shorter milestones so you can navigate and adjust and / OR grab someone who's been there before to show the way.
2. Don't focus on obstacles or you will hit them look ahead to where you want to be (over and over)

Photo Dave Thomas...
visit his gallery

Perseverance

In order to get better, to produce, succeed you have to put in the time. You may fall, take some significant knocks that will cause you to lay awake at night in a sweat (see: pulled back muscles or overextended debt) Perseverance should be part of your plan and mind set from the start, tell yourself it will get better, reach out to others for support and be prepared at times to reach deep.

You may think it is done having achieved the black diamond status.. but if you are truly in the zone it is never done.

Yes it gets easier but there will still be days of keeping up with the faster better skiers , the kids, climbing the last meters of an ascent or a decent when you are absolutely sure a lung is about to burst. Or that the staff, your brain and patience is going to expire. Making it those last few hundred meters can be the difference between a good and bad day..and achieving your end goals...

"Success is not final, failure is not fatal: it is the courage to continue that counts."

—Winston Churchill

Photo Jordan Manley
www.jordanmanley.com

Life is too short... work to make your business passionate and joyful for you, your staff and customers. And your skiing days should always be great = because you are skiing.

"You should never be too old, too busy or too serious to do something good for the soul. "

Joy

And /or bliss, pride, fun, satisfaction... I am one of the lucky ones who can achieve the same level of joy innovating and in my work business coaching as I do skiing...

Some joy sources? The perfect line that is all yours..or farmed with a friend, listening to the reverberating hoots and hollers of other joyous skiers. In business this can be the joy of team accomplishments, achieving milestones, network/industry celebrations etc.

Take a moment of reflection in the midst of it all to recognize where you are, what you have accomplished, the opportunities that lie ahead and just be happy about it. Business or skiing –we don't do this enough... look back at those tracks and be proud... Look ahead and rejoice how lucky we are for this moment and opportunity.

As business owners we rarely take a moment to truly celebrate and recognize what we have accomplished.

The underlying sense of fulfillment in our activities should be a constant energizer for us to continue to break trail and break through the barriers we perceive in our way...

Share your keys to
joy in business on the site:
www.liftbusinesscoaching.com

"Leadership is the art of getting someone else to do something you want done because he wants to do it."

—Dwight Eisenhower

Team

Surround yourself with people who inspire, educate, support, energize and bring a dash of reality.

Ski with those who push you sometimes; who by following you gain confidence and skills.

Ski with those at your level of skiing and sometimes ski with those you can mentor.

Your team roster whether skiing or business can be eclectic and supportive, comprised of different strengths and aptitudes bringing different value in different conditions. (see: powder day ski partner vs. relaxed sunny day groomer ski partner)

Your work team may include immediate staff but don't forget advisors, mentors, family and other supporters.

Celebrate and foster positive energy and let the leaders lead, take some time to follow and see where it goes...

You can't call every line every time. Trust and empower your crew; you just might find lines and opportunities you hadn't even thought of.

And for goodness sake keep folks excited about what they are doing, celebrate and have fun when you can.

Photo: Lawrence
www.lawrencewrightphoto.com

Skier team on route to very serious competition last day of skiing Red Mountain Resort BC

Mentors, coaches & your team

Grab some assurance and hang on...

For goodness sake reach out, take the short rope and rappel when you need it!

Spending a focused, goal orientated session with folks who have the mad skills and experience can save you so much time, pain and uncertainty.

You COULD learn to ski or mountaineer from a book or on your own.. but it would be frustrating painful , DANGEROUS and so inefficient... so why do we try to solo it so often in business??

Even if it is just a short one off to learn a particular skill (skiing or business)

– reach out! Check resources on www.liftbusinesscoaching.com for a resource list and community chat to share programs (many are free ;)

Photographer Ace Kvale embodies supporting others from his start as ski model, to world class photographer to now using his skills to support communities and people worldwide in need .. please visit his site to view his humanitarian projects and as always view his amazing photography http://acekvale.com
In this photo: Anne Smith on Ama Dablam, Nepal

Women can

Don't forget the most important 50% rule

Do I have to say it ? ...in skiing and business...

Woman can rock it.

To overlook that is to overlook half of your potential team, staff, mentorship, partners and more...

For sales and marketing: this demographic is the primary decision maker for purchases...

If your organization has a good ratio WTG If you don't... take a look at why?

To the women out there – continue to change how things are done on skis, business and otherwise... push boundaries, celebrate and of course where ever possible have fun out there.

Photo by Marko Shapiro `Master of Light` - ski industry photography icon providing us great photos from the 70`s to date in publications worldwide ...visit MarkShapiro.com for more incredible photos

Skier : Stephanie Gauvin Location: Red Mountain Resort, Rossland BC Canada (authors fav ski terrain)

Target Market

Don't bet that if you build it they will come

I LOVE start ups and product developers. I love the love they have for ideas. They are my tribe.

And we share a condition I call Widet-itis My <fill blank> does such amazing things And they generally do.. do amazing things.

But the killer is (ok it is skiing and this is COLD)

Who cares?

And do they care enough to pay your asking price?

Because unless you have identified who will use and value your product enough to pay for itself 10 fold .....

You may be running on empty

"No enterprise can exist for itself alone. It ministers to some great need, it performs some great service, not for itself, but for others.. or failing therein, it ceases to be profitable and ceases to exist."

—Calvin Coolidge

Photo: Sophie Wong
http://sophiewongphotography.com

Ladies circa 20's... bold.
Photo www.VintageWinter.com

There are a couple points to be made about skiing, business and gear. The ski gear story is a very valid lesson in business, competition, survival and evolution of better products for consumers.

Opportunities to compete are accelerating new technologies, global marketplace and other factors can allow you to really evolve to the needs of your target market quickly... provide value to your clients & help them soar

Product Evolution

Love the cutting edge...

I do not doubt that if the snowboard had remained quarantined to Mt Baker (where I skied in part in the early 80's) instead of breaking down the bans, going mainstream and proving itself easier to learn than skiing; that skis would still be neon, 200 cm long and 1.5 inches wide. Let alone the beauty 7 ft skis wood skis in the pic to the left Competition is often the necessity of a radical product changes and brand opportunities.

By year 2000 the 100% market share of the undisputed king of snow (aka skis) was sliding to snowboards with a 30% + and rising market share gouge. But some in the ski industry saw an opportunity and they nailed it. Thanks goodness...and goddess. And new ski manufacturers rose out of the storm to take a good % of their industry share shaking up the more complacent ski producers by producing better performing shape skis. And I will thank them on every turn for the rest of my ski days ...

Be the visionary, see the market gaps, opportunities and take your customers and company to the next level ...

www.skilogik.com

A green, killer ski with social kickback while you lean back and enjoy the ride

King of the world - information

It is like winning the lotto..

the perfect call...
booking a ski trip
heading out for a day
tour launching a new
product when the
market is ready.

The world is your oyster.

There is no excuse
anymore.
If you want the
weather forecast or ski
conditions they are
online in real time...

In business tap your
market online in social
media. Follow the
industry news in online
feeds.

There are no excuses to
not be brimming with
the latest info on what
you need. In skiing and
business there is still an
element of "follow you
gut" maybe based on
wind direction to get to
loaded snow or sensing
a tipping point on the
horizon. But there has
never been such a flow
of available intel to
make decisions...

Viva technology (segue
to next page)

Image via www.snowseekers.ca
providers of Western Canadian ski
conditions &resort intel / deals online

Technology

I love to ski ... I work virtually for the majority of my jobs.

So I work from the chairlift on my waterproof iPhone. Every day I spend some time to research and test new apps. Here's a few tidbits to bring this idea home:

In 2010 5 trillion texts were exchanged. Over a billion iPhone apps downloaded Facebook has 800+ mill citizens.

(I have a presentation on working at speed of light and am very aware of the expanding rate of intel online..)

Please don't ignore technology

It is changing EVERYTHING from the ski gear you wear to how you do business.

Find out how it can help you and adopt it... (not all of it for gods sake) just the aspects that will suit your business. It is enormously relevant. ..

And use it to continue to evolve your business to be the best it can be.

Visit goo.gl/2Mc3f for a few ski apps for fun and a gem a day ;)

If you are an adventure tour company check www.adventureengine.com for tech solutions - discount for readers of this book on the book website!

In photo: Natasha of Betty Go Hard – dedicated to women in action sports online community and camps http://bettygohard.ca

Balance says it all ..

respect the elements of
your life that make you
the best you can be and
avoid letting one eclipse
the others to your
detriment.. it's a roller
coaster but be aware ...
and seek the balance
that will make your life a
great one.

Balance

Photo by Elina Sirparanta
www.elinaphoto.com

This is just a start to all the possible parallels between business and skiing and I look forward to conversations on more from my reader community online.

I dedicate this book to all the folks out there skiing, working and striving to achieve nirvana. To those start ups – launch it!

I wish to all of you great powder days, good comrades in skiing and work. That you continue to forge a path to the goals you have made and to the success and joy you deserve. Have some fun out there!

Love your dream... work your line and launch it

Photo: Francois Marseille: action sport photographer based in BC Kootenays
http://goo.gl/CR3Ms

This black and white square is a QR code with a smart phone
1. download a "QR reader"
2. focus it on the code & it will take you to the website of the photographer on the page

Being a skier and new technology lover I thought this would be a fun way to share our worlds... good business & ski to all... and of course if you want information on using QR for your products there is an info sheet on this campaign at www.liftbusiness.com

Visit www.liftbusinescoaching.com for:
- forums relating to this book and a community chat area for skiers and starts ups alike
- discount coupon codes to local cat ski operations - business resources

And of course feel free to contact us about arranging a skiing business trip to BC Canada, business coaching and or consulting.

Have an adventure tourism business or interest?

Your industry news and technology solution is available at www. adventureengine.com

Visit #1 LinkedIn group for adventure tourism and travel professionals at www.linkedin.com/groups/ Adventure-Tourism-Travel-Professionals-1926114 to join 5,000+ in business discussions and adventure opportunities

For additional resources such as Top 10 start up rules, start up community / book forums visit Liftbusinesscoaching.com

Twitter: Facebook:

More ski resources and links

www.liftbusinesscoaching.com

Contributor biographies

Author/compiler:

Amber Hayes www.liftbusinesscoaching.com		Amber is a serial entrepreneur and skier typically on Red Mountain (for at least an hour a day) while working on the chair lift with her smartphone. An international coaching federation member, software company owner, speaker, mentor, coach and consultant for innovation and new tech in businesses she skis the ski she talks. And she thanks the photographers in the book for making this project possible and reminds readers to visit contributor sites and to ski, work live large!

Photographers:

Another several pages could be dedicated to the photographers in this book. This following line up includes industry veterans who have literally shaped ski photography, newcomers, specialists and all of them go to great lengths in every sense of business, ski , life and limb and very soul to capture amazing shots and allow us to celebrate our sport.

Thank you for your dedication to your work and to allowing us to experience the amazing moments in skiing you share with us...

Ace Kvale www.acekvale.com http://goo.gl/aVEOU		Photographer Ace Kvale embodies supporting others from his start as ski model, to world class photographer to now using his skills to support communities and people worldwide in need… please visit his site to view his humanitarian projects… and as always his amazing photography
Christian Pondella www.christianpondella.com goo.gl/xlExc		Christian Pondella is an adventure sports photographer based in Mammoth Lakes, CA. As a participant in a lot of the activities he shoots, he likes to get close to the action, " I want the viewer to feel like they are right there in the photo, show them a perspective they might not ever see on there own." "Note from author of this book "I chose Christians shots for this reason + the confidence and commitment clearly demonstrated to get the shot- inspiring!"

Dave Thomas http://unreddave.smugmug.com goo.gl/K7a11		Photographer living in the Kootenay region of BC Dave captured small town in big mountains, was a photographer for local ski operations & is now the manager for Baldface Cat ski lodge. Dave still enjoys shooting the mountain scenes and snow riders whenever possible.
Elina Sirparanta www.elinaphoto.com goo.gl/mHK6X		Even though I am specialized in action photography and especially freestyle skiing, I have had the chance to explore more and more other domains of photography and enjoy capturing people, emotions and expressions, imagining scenes and making images out of that.
Francois Marseille goo.gl/CR3Ms		
Jordan Manely www.jordanmanley.com goo.gl/iJaa7		"For the second year in a row, photographer Jordan Manley - a frequent contributor to Skiing magazine - has taken the top honors at Whistler's Deep Winter Photo Challenge. We're not surprised. Manley is having a career year. He bagged the covers of both Powder and Skiing..and he snared a disproportionate number of pages in our December Best Photos of the Year gallery…- Skiing mag
Lawrence Wright www.blowup.ca goo.gl/RW6zR		

Marko Shapiro www.markoshapiro.com goo.gl/ZZYvz		Labelled by Powder Magazine as the Godfather of Ski photography as the Master of Light by Snow magazine (France) Mark Shapiros work has influenced ski photography from the 70's to current day (one of his latest shots included in this book). He has even been awarded a medal by the Ski Club of Great Britain for his contribution to ski editorial and the winter Sports industry.
Sophie Wong www.sophiewongphotography.com goo.gl/NlClR		Custom photographer located in Rossland BC. I specialize in natural light family portraiture, sports and lifestyle photography. In winter she can also be found perched amongst terrain to capture free ski shots during competitions or just for fun.
SnowSeekers www.snowseekers.ca goo.gl/T8SMG		SnowSeekers is the a snow-minded new-media company that delivers incredible videos, informative articles, and stellar photos through SnowSeekers.ca, SnowSeekers TV, and a line of smartphone applications. Whether it's for die hard locals, vacationing families, or powderhounds from across the globe, SnowSeekers highlights all the amazing snowbound opportunities in Alberta and BC.

Designer:

Jana Rade www.impactstudiosonline.com goo.gl/8NqMU		Jana is a graphic designer with passion for working on books and editorial design. She's been in the business for 16 years and runs her own graphic design studio from lovely Ontario, Canada.

www.ingramcontent.com/pod-product-compliance
Lightning Source LLC
Chambersburg PA
CBHW041452210326
41599CB00004B/224